When you can't fin
Create One!

Bill Effinger

New Century Publishing

100 E. San Marcos Blvd. Suite 400

San Marcos, CA 92069

First E-Book edition September 2011

With contribution from Roxanne Rapske

ISBN-13: 978-0615537962

DEDICATION

This book is dedicated to the 14 Million unemployed Americans currently searching for work.

There's nothing worse than being unemployed unless it's being unemployed along with 13,999,999 others and not being able to find a job. If that's the situation you are in, and I assume you are, or you wouldn't have chosen this book.

This book is also dedicated to the American tradition of creative ingenuity and entrepreneurial individualism which has always been the driving force behind our country's economic engine.

CONTENTS

About the Author

Bill Effinger has several decades of hands-on experience as a developer; builder of homes and commercial projects; mortgage lender; sales; leasing; forward planning consultant and land acquisition specialist. As the Former Mayor of Buena Park California Bill Helped sponsor the first American student participation in President Eisenhower's People to People Program. A long time member of the NAHB, Bill was an appointed member of the National Marketing Committee, National Education Chairman of the Remodelers' Council and has had many of his cogent industry related articles on marketing and management published in the NAHB Business Journal, National Association of Realtors Magazine, Boston Business Journal, and Builder Magazine.

Bill has been a guest lecturer on the subject of entrepreneurism at several colleges and universities, among them, Babson and MIT in Boston, Arizona State and National University. Published locally and nationally, Bill has also been a building industry seminar leader in various cities. He created a successful twelve week course for the Greater Boston Building Association entitled "How to Survive, Succeed and Grow in the Building & Contracting Business" and is Publisher/Editor of the San Diego Commercial Real Estate News Newsletter: http://www.sandiegocommercialnews.com

Bill has authored four books and a course syllabus on business planning and marketing for the Greater Boston Building Association.

The first book was published in 1995, titled "Making Crime Pay-How Identity Thieves steal your money" which predicted the pandemic of identity theft so prevalent today. The second was an 80-year retrospective of his life in 2010, and the third is titled "The Vortex made me do it" a historical and satirical record of Desert Hot Springs California.

Bill resides in San Marcos California with his wife Diana. Together, they have six children, sixteen grand children and eight great-grand children. Bill maintains his consulting office in the City Hall complex of San Marcos, continuing to serve his Affordable Housing developer clients.

****

When you can't find a JOB-Create one!

ACKNOWLEDGMENTS

My most sincere thanks to the many friends, business associates and family members who took the time and interest to assist me in putting this book together and for putting up with the frantic pace of which I forced on everyone. But in my view, the effort to "strike while the iron is hot" with the unemployment topic now front and center in our nation is essential to the success of the book and the unemployed needing help. For that, I offer my apology.

To the participants listed on the closing pages of the book who gave of their time in sharing their personal experiences in starting and operating a small business, your words of encouragement to the many who will be following your example is very valuable, and I thank you.

To my son Kirk, a gifted writer and freelance columnist whose work appears regularly in the *North County Times* newspaper for his always expert editing of my sentence structure and grammar. And to my son Lynn, a published author of "Believe to Achieve", for his meticulous editing.

To my son-in-law Glenn Karrmann and our daughter Linda Karrmann for their continuous support, encouragement and researching the contents of the "For Our Veterans" pages and Health Care pages. As a retired Navy Veteran and current Educator, Glenn knows the difficulties our Veterans face when reentering the working world and Linda, a Human Recourses executive who is extremely knowledgeable in that field.

Last in order, but first in her loyalty to me, is my life partner and wife Diana who listens to my ideas, critiquing them honestly and keeping me on the right path; for her encouragement as she tirelessly read and re-read the manuscript in its many forms, but mostly for her love and understanding of my very early morning work habits.

Thank You All!

INTRODUCTION

There's nothing worse than being unemployed unless it's being unemployed along with 13,999,999 others and not being able to find a job. If that's the situation you are in, and I assume you are, or you wouldn't have picked up this book, then creating a job for yourself may be the answer for you.

As unique individuals, each of us has unique experiences and capabilities we have learned during our lifetime in school and working for/with others. Capitalizing on the uniqueness of your experiences and then sharing them with others to help them become better managers and business operators while earning an income from your effort is what this book is about.

The standing joke is that if you are a "Consultant" you are unemployed. I'm here to tell you that I am a consultant and have been employed as such for many years. My hours are flexible. My income is relatively higher than average. I can and do choose whom I wish to work with. The work is gratifying and fulfilling, with less stress than I have had managing my own businesses or when managing a public company, and I have no employees to be responsible for or to. Life is good.

I am not proposing that everyone should become a consultant. However, everyone has something they can do better than someone else. The secret is finding that something, honing and perfecting your expertise and turning it into your own money machine.

We are born with basic skill sets and there are learned skill sets which we obtain from various activities and jobs we have held while growing up.

I consider myself fortunate to have grown up during the depression years after the First World War. Times were tough for everyone and I was doing odd jobs at a very early age to earn my own spending money. Then when my dad was killed when I was thirteen, my working became essential, as there was just my mom, my eight-year old brother and me to make our way in the world. As a result, by the time I was seventeen and entering the U.S.

Navy, I was a few steps ahead of many of my shipmates which paid off in many ways that I demonstrate later in the book.

There is a section of the book that asks you to delve into your past, and list all of the things you have done that required some type of learned or natural skills, whether it was an actual job, a household chore that was your responsibility or something you learned to do in school.

There are things you enjoy doing and there are things you don't. They should all go into your "inventory". Out of your initial list, you will find the one area where you have the expertise to succeed in being self-employed, making an income in the process. By so doing, you will be creating your own job.

So let's get started. Pick up a pencil and paper or power up your laptop and start putting together your personal inventory. Once that's completed, walk through and study the following pages of this book, making notes at the end of each section where provided, so the book will become a working manual for your future.

I have placed a positive affirmation at the bottom of each note-page to help you declare your commitment to this process and reaching your goal of self employment.

As your coach, I will be with you all the way. Should you have a quick question, just go to the web site: www.createmyjob.org and click on the "Hey Coach" tab; fill out the form and write-"I have a question" and I will respond within 48-hours. I am also available for extended coaching sessions for a fee.

I am proud to say that over the past fifty years I have mentored several individuals who have since become successful business owners and some, millionaires, all of whom I can count as friends. My goal is to help set you on the same path.

Now, let's get on with your new life as a self employed small business person.

Jump in! The water's fine!

You are better than you think you are

This past July, I was given the honor of delivering the Commencement address to the graduating class of Vincennes University's North Island Naval Air Station where I had been stationed in 1947 and 1948. Part of that address, was my Ten Commandments for Success which I have adhered to my entire career. When followed, you can't go wrong.

Ten Commandments for Success

1.) Never give up.

Solving a problem or overcoming adversity is difficult, but rarely impossible. It has been said that when the going gets tough, the tough get going.

2.) Explore every opportunity.

Opportunity is knocking every day in numerous ways. Keep your eyes open for how you might make the world better through your innovative instincts.

3.) Treat failure as a learning experience.

Thomas Edison declared after his 1000th failed experiment in attempting to create an incandescent light bulb, that "Now I know a thousand ways how not to make a light bulb".

4.) Never fear the unknown.

Take a chance. Have confidence in yourself. Every new product on the shelf, in your garage or on your desk has emanated out of its creator being courageous enough to say "what if?"

5.) Welcome change.

Our world is changing as we stand here this morning. Stay in sync with the dynamics of change. More to the point "go with the flow" but at all times maintain your basic values and use common sense—something there is not enough of these days.

6.) Treat others as you wish to be treated.

We can't expect not to be lied to or cheated, if we lie or cheat. What goes around comes around, so stay honest and honorable.

7.) Admit your mistakes.

We all make them, so why try to run away from them? Figure out what went wrong and then move on accepting blame, thereby being accountable for your actions.

8.) Believe in the power of positive thinking.

Dr. Norman Vincent Peale wrote the book on this subject, and believe me, it works. Always looking at life as a glass half-full, constantly sets the stage for your future accomplishments.

9.) Believe in yourself.

If you don't believe in yourself, why should anyone else? Have belief in your own convictions. Fight hard for what you think is right until and unless there is solid provable evidence you may be wrong. Should you be wrong, then be strong enough to admit it.

10) Always remember: Attitude is everything.

Enthusiasm is contagious and projects an upbeat attitude in everything you do and onto everyone you interact with. Your

attitude is the first thing you project personally or on the phone. Be genuinely interested in listening and learning.

Live your life to the fullest and never look back. We can't undo yesterday, but we can make a better tomorrow. And pledge to give back to the world what it has given you. Making a better day for someone less fortunate than you, will never get old.

Listen to yourself. You are better and smarter than you think you are.

I WILL MAKE THIS WORK FOR ME BY:

Blank Space for your notes

AFFIRMATION: Today I firmly take charge of myself.

To prove it, let's do a little self analysis

About a year ago, one of my clients asked me to do a one-day "Boot Camp" for some of her key consultants and employees. Some of the content of that Boot Camp applies at this point in the book, so here goes:

Personal Character & Commitment Exercise

This is a self analysis of what you consider to be your strengths and weaknesses in attaining your short and long term personal and business goals. You are expected to be honest with yourself.

I have a Life Plan: Yes No If yes it is in writing: Yes No

I am Goal Oriented: Yes No

I am Competitive in: Some Most All things I do: Yes No

I consider myself a leader in my daily and social activities Yes No

I am doing what I love & I love what I do: Yes No

I consider myself responsible and pro-active in political issues: Yes No

I belong to, and am active in professional organizations: Yes No

I am an Over-achiever: Yes No Average: Yes No

I am a problem solver: Yes No

I enjoy a challenge: Yes No

I enjoy__________________the most of what I do Daily.

I enjoy___________________the least in what I do Daily

My__________________is first in my life

I believe my life is balanced: Yes No

I would_____________if an opportunity presented itself

I am: Satisfied Unsatisfied Dissatisfied with my current Social life

I am: Satisfied Unsatisfied Dissatisfied with my current Work life

I am: Satisfied Unsatisfied Dissatisfied with my current Family life

I am: Organized Unorganized Disorganized in my daily work habits

If I were King, I would:

Blank Space for your notes

AFFIRMATION: I am determined to follow through until I am finished.

Patton's Principles for Managers/Owners who mean it Title & list **from the book by Porter B. Williamson**

I was 11 years old when Pearl Harbor was bombed, and I became an avid fan of General George Patton through the newspapers and RKO Radio News in the movies and on the radio. His advice is worth a sincere look. Whether you agree with him or not isn't the point. He makes you think—that's the point.

Please check the following as to whether you Agree or Disagree:

1. Keep a quick line of communication: Agree Disagree
2. Say what you mean, mean what you say: Agree Disagree
3. Any man (or woman) that thinks he/she is indispensable, ain't: Agree Disagree
4. The mission is all important—think of standard rules later: Agree Disagree
5. Always be alert to the source of trouble: Agree Disagree
6. Select leaders for accomplishment, not for Affection: Agree Disagree
7. To gain strength, always go beyond exhaustion: Agree Disagree
8. Never fear failure: Agree Disagree
9. Talk with the "troops" Agree Disagree
10. No one is thinking if everyone is thinking alike: Agree Disagree
11. Know what you know and know what you don't know: Agree Disagree
12. Never make a decision too early or too late: Agree Disagree

13. The way to win is never to lose; Agree Disagree

14. Success is how high you bounce on the bottom: Agree Disagree

15. Always keep something in reserve: Agree Disagree

Now, please rearrange the above list in their order of priority as you see them in your every day life. Should you disagree with any of these Principles, write a note to yourself here and talk it out with your spouse and friends to get their perspective.

Your world won't collapse on any of the answers you have given here. It's just a way to get to know yourself a little better.

I disagree/agree and here's why:

Blank Space for your notes

Stephen Covey wrote an excellent book a few years back titled **"The Seven Habits of Highly effective People"**

Listed below are the seven habits. Please write a brief statement on how you might, or already do use this advice in your work and play.

- Habit 1: Be Proactive:
- Habit 2: Begin with the end in mind:
- Habit 3: Put First Things First:
- Habit 4: Think Win Win:
- Habit 5: Seek First to Understand, Then to be understood:
- Habit 6: Synergize:
- Habit 7: Sharpen the Saw:

Remember, these are just exercises to get your mind moving in the direction of where you want to go as you become acclimated to becoming self employed, nobody is grading you. You are getting better acquainted with you here.

I already apply Habit Number(s)

Blank Space for your notes

I may apply Habit Number (s) in the future because:

Blank Space for your notes

"The only thing we have to fear is fear itself"

That statement was delivered by the 32nd President of the United States, Franklin D. Roosevelt during the depths of the depression in 1932 when unemployment was a coincidental 14 Million and a staggering 25% of the workforce (twice what it is today by percentage). Interestingly at the same time, a new magazine was launched successfully that is still being published today.

Fortune magazine was to have been put on the stands at a price of 10 cents a copy. However, the printer made a major error and the staggering price of $1.00 was boldly imprinted on the cover. What to do? The publisher took a chance. The magazines were placed at all of the newsstands in New York and they were snapped up more quickly than any magazine had ever experienced before it.

What was the analysis of this in retrospect? Everyone figured if this new magazine was that expensive, it must have had some very valuable information and was worth the money.

Why did I put that story here? Because the lesson is that you are as valuable as you make yourself to be in the market you are in. Just because your last job paid you $40 an hour doesn't mean you can't charge three times that amount for the expertise you have which is needed by someone that doesn't have it. You are worth what you think you are.

I WILL MAKE THIS WORK FOR ME BY:

Blank Space for your notes

AFFIRMATION: Today I take the first steps toward my goal.

Believe in Yourself

That's my ninth commandment and worth repeating: If you don't believe in yourself, why should anyone else? Have belief in your own convictions. Fight hard for what you think is right until and unless there is solid provable evidence you may be wrong. Should you be wrong, then be strong enough to admit it and move on.

I WILL MAKE THIS WORK FOR ME BY:

Blank Space for your notes

AFFIRMATION: I believe in myself and my ability to achieve great results.

Ignore the Nay-Sayers

And there will be many. "This is being irresponsible" "Who's going to use your services/buy your product?" "You don't have enough money" "Nobody will think you're serious" "Times are too tough" "Keep looking, you will find a job" are just a few of the 'don't do this" comments you will hear. Ignore them.

History is full of stories of successful business people who were discouraged from venturing into the unknown. History has proven the nay-Sayers to be wrong. Many industry giants of today were started during a recession or depression, Microsoft being one.

Researching for this book, I found this posting on Google:

14 Big Businesses That Started in a Recession

By Sarah Caron

It might seem counterintuitive to start a new business when the economy is in the dumps. But a recession can actually be the ideal time for launching a company. In fact, many well-known and successful organizations were born during an economic slump.

Why do these companies succeed? Usually it's because the founders recognized a market need and filled it. Identifying that need — whether it's related to entertainment, travel or even streamlining how businesses operate — is the key to any thriving enterprise, regardless of the economic climate in which it begins. The following major corporations made it big during recessions by doing just that.

Hyatt Corp. opened its first hotel's doors at the Los Angeles International Airport during the Eisenhower recession (1957 to 1958). The chain rose to worldwide fame in the following decades and now operates more than 365 hotels in 25 countries with premium services such as wifi hotspots.

Burger King Corp., with its flame-broiled burgers, is another recession startup. The company began in 1954 when James McLamore and David Edgerton opened a Burger King restaurant in Miami, Fla. During another recession in 1957, the company introduced its successful signature burger — the Whopper. Today, the company operates more than 11,100 locations in 65 countries.

IHOP Corp. is another star from the Eisenhower recession. The first restaurant in the now national chain opened its doors July1958 in Toluca Lake, Calif. Owners Al and Jerry Lapin were at the helm of the fast growing company, which began franchising just three years later. Today, there are more than 1,300 locations across the U.S.

The Jim Henson Company was created by famed puppeteer Jim Henson in 1958. Henson's business was responsible for some of the best-known puppet characters of all time including Miss Piggy, Kermit the Frog and Elmo. Today, the privately held company is managed by Henson's children and continues to thrive by creating popular kids-friendly shows and movies.

LexisNexis is a research hub for the law, media and more. The company, originally a government contractor, began its LexisNexis computerized legal research service during the 1973 oil crisis that rocked the country into steep economic slump. The now Web-based service is used in 100 countries by individuals in law, government, education and business.

FedEx Corp. began operations on April 17, 1973 as Federal Express, a nod to the Federal Reserve, with whom founder Frederick W.

Smith had hoped to get a contract. He didn't, but the company that delivered 186 packages to 25 cities on its first night of operations now manages more than 7.5 million shipments everyday worldwide.

Microsoft Corp. wasn't always the jaw-dropping enterprise it is today. In 1975, when it was created by Harvard University dropout Bill Gates, Microsoft was just a little company in Albuquerque, N.M. It dealt in rudimentary computing languages and began its climb to business stardom with the success of MS-DOS, which was sold and marketed to IBM Corp. and then-IBM clones. Today, the company is estimated to earn more than $60 billion in revenue per year and is branching into new areas including VoIP and CRM.

CNN might be a news giant now, but in recession-plagued 1980, it was a little-known station called The Cable Network News. It revolutionized how people received information when it premiered as the first 24-hour all-news channel. Today, 1.5 billion people across the globe watch CNN.

MTV Networks brought something new and different to the music scene when it debuted in the economic slump of 1981. Intended to be an all-music-video channel, MTV used VJs (video jockeys) to host programs and facilitate transitions between videos. Today, MTV is a global brand with dozens of shows, music-related and not.

Trader Joe's started as a chain of convenience stores called Pronto Markets in the slow financial times of 1958. In 1967, the company changed its name to Trader Joe's and began to carry unique grocery items under its own brand. The company now operates more than 280 stores in the U.S.

Wikipedia Foundation Inc. was born during the recent post-9/11 recession. Established in January 2001, the online encyclopedia had more than 100,000 entries by 2003. Today it is home to more than

2.5 million articles and continues to grow.

Sports Illustrated magazine was launched on August 16, 1954, at the tail-end of a recession. The magazine benefitted from fortunate timing as a boom in professional sports exploded soon after its founding. Sports Illustrated now sells about 3 million copies in the U.S. each week.

GE (General Electric Co.) was established in 1876 by famed American inventor Thomas Edison. In the middle of the Panic of 1873, a six-year recession, Edison created one of the best-known inventions of all time — the incandescent light bulb. In terms of market capitalization, GE is now the third largest company in the world. The enterprise has evolved from a manufacturing-strong business to an enterprise earning more than 50 percent of its revenue from its financial services division.

HP (Hewlett-Packard Development Company LP) was inauspiciously born in a Palo Alto garage at the end of the Great Depression. The electronic company, initially supported by a mere $538 investment, has grown into the first technology business to exceed $100 billion in revenue, earning $104 billion in 2007. It now operates in nearly every country in the world.

Recessions, however, aren't advantageous only to start-ups. Pre-existing companies can also make incredible gains in years where the economy is down. Some of the most recent success stories are those of Google, PayPal and Salesforce.com Inc. From 2000 to 2001 each of these companies thrived, leading PayPal to go public in 2002, followed by Google and Salesforce.com in 2004.

****

Those examples are some pretty impressive reasons for you to go for it—don't you think? Even if you aren't planning on becoming the next Trader Joes or

FedEx, the above examples clearly show that down-times can become up-times, with ideas and hard work.

The last section of this book contains some words of encouragement from people I have been fortunate to have been associated with during my lifetime. Each of them have started and grown at least one successful company and some, more than one.

Please read their words of wisdom and encouragement. They will settle your nerves and help you gain support from your family and friends as you launch your new life.

I WILL MAKE THIS WORK FOR ME by:

Blank Space for your notes

AFFIRMATION: My life has infinite possibilities.

What's to lose?

You aren't working now and jobs are near impossible to find, right?

Look, nothing says that as you are planning your new venture of self employment, you can't also be looking for a job. Allocate a portion of your day to job-seeking and a portion to planning your self-employment strategies. That should satisfy those closest to you who are concerned for your welfare. Planning your days and weeks is an import element in the life of the self-employed anyway, so making a time schedule is good business practice for your future.

I WILL MAKE THIS WORK FOR ME BY:

Blank Space for your notes

AFFIRMATION: I am willing to risk; to put it all on the line.

The only way is up!

When looking for a job hasn't provided anything for you, what's wrong with inventorying your physical and mental assets and sorting through them to create your own job, doing what you enjoy and making a reasonable living at it? ABSOLUTLEY NOTHING! When you're on the bottom, the only way is up!

I WILL MAKE THIS WORK FOR ME BY:

Blank Space for your notes

AFFIRMATION: I learn from every situation I encounter.

Now let's do your Personal Inventory

Your past job(s) and experience(s)

With paper and pencil in hand, or on your laptop, start your list, going as far back as you can remember, writing down experiences and jobs you have had as they come to mind. Don't worry about putting them in order just yet, you can do that later. Just keep putting everything down that comes to mind.

Once you have completed the list, make a trailing note after those jobs/experiences you liked and why, and those you didn't like and why.

With this exercise completed, using a scale of 1 to 10, rate each. When you have rated them all, move the top five to a new page and set it aside.

MY PAST JOBS AND EXPERIENCES:

Blank Space for your notes

What you like to do

Now that we have a list of the top five things you like to do and why you like to do them, let's find out how we can narrow them down to what you will be most likely to earn a self-employment income from.

WHAT I LIKE TO DO:

Blank Space for your notes

What you are good at

Once again go to the page of the top five jobs/experiences you like to do; then using a 1 to 10 scale, rate these five and put them in order. With that completed, select the top two and put them on a separate page. Now we have two potential self-employment opportunities to consider, and it's time to get serious and review a couple of basic issues.

WHAT I AM GOOD AT:

Blank Space for your notes

AFFIRMATION: I am proud of my achievements.

Your savings if any—Hint: Not having any savings isn't a deal killer.

Assuming you have some savings, the accounts are being depleted as you try to find a job. Setting up a self-employment strategy isn't going to deplete your savings any faster, but it may get you to some income a lot quicker.

On the other hand, if you have no savings, you are no worse off planning for self-employment, than you were just looking for a job. Some people will say "but you must stay focused". That may be true to a certain extent, but in the multi-task world we live in, you must be able to focus on more than one thing at the same time. Sometimes even three or four things.

The bottom line is, that if you have savings, that will help you some, but no more or less than if you just continue to look for a job.

I WILL MAKE THIS WORK FOR ME BY:

Blank Space for your notes

AFFIRMATION: Today I am rich because I am courageous.

Your credit: Good? Average? Poor?

Here again, most people who have been out of work for a period of time, have run up credit card debt to survive and as a result, their FICO scores have taken a hit. Should the credit card payments slide, then it's a Catch 22; the interest is piling up and the cards are cut off. Not to worry. You are no worse off if this is your situation while you are looking for a job, than if you are planning your self-employment.

When you have good or average credit, and you can use that as a backup, of course that's a good thing. But poor or bad credit isn't the end of your dreams; it just makes the hill a little harder to climb.

I WILL MAKE THIS WORK FOR ME BY:

Blank Space for your notes

AFFIRMATION: I deserve to be prosperous and successful.

Make a Plan

O.K. now we're starting to get serious here. It's time to build your new business---don't forget, self-employment is a business. You may not have employees and you may not have an office or rented shop, but you are a business person nevertheless. Good businesses start with a good plan and succeed when the plan is followed.

There is a common but misguided notion that putting a plan to paper is constricting and rigid. ***NOT TRUE!*** A good business plan is flexible and easy to meld into changing economic times and markets similar to what we are experiencing now. Right from the start, your plan should be adjustable to help you succeed, as you will see.

Several years ago, I produced a seminar titled: "How to Survive, Succeed & Grow in the Building and Contracting Business" for the Greater Boston Building Association. The syllabus provided for ten three-hour sessions, which when completed, the participants had a complete business and marketing plan and the cost was $395.00. Not a small sum for small contractors, but very inexpensive when considering what it would cost to have a plan designed by an independent consultant.

Today, my fee would be anywhere from $2,500 to $5,000 for such a plan.

We had 45 participants and when completed, we received rave reviews from my client, the Greater Boston Building Association and from the Boston Business Journal. I mention this because of the importance of a good plan and following the plan to help you succeed, as boring or unnecessary as you may think it might be. So..........

What Is a Business Plan?

A business plan is any plan that works for a business to look ahead, allocate resources, focus on key points, and prepare for problems and opportunities. *Business planning is about results.* Your plan should match your purpose.

Unfortunately, many people think of business plans only for starting a new business or applying for business loans. *But business plans are also vital for running a business,* whether or not the business needs new loans or new investments. Businesses need plans to *optimize growth and development according to priorities.*

Building your business on paper before you open your wallet will make eminent sense to you as you ply the waters of self-employment. Believe me!

What a Business Plan is ***NOT***

- **A Business Plan is NOT rigid**
- **A Business Plan is NOT final**
- **A Business Plan is NOT unchangeable**
- **A Business Plan is NOT about "rules"**

I WILL MAKE THIS WORK FOR ME BY:

Blank Space for your notes

AFFIRMATION: Today I am able to see the big picture.

Put down on paper what you plan to do and how you will proceed

Grab that pencil and paper again, or put the laptop in front of you and let's get started. At the top of the page in bold letters, write: **MY SELF- EMPLOYMENT PLAN** (you can pick a real name or your business title later)

I have provided pages at the end of the book for you to transfer your completed self employment plan to, so you can use the book as a working Diary/Manual for your reference and profitable enjoyment in future years.

Describe your vision for your self-employment enterprise. You can be as expansive in this as you wish as it's a good way to flesh out your thoughts for what you are intending to do with the rest of your life. We call this the: **Executive Summary**.

Once you have the description completed (you will probably return to this many times, adjusting, tweaking and changing things before you have completed your plan) set it aside, and start building a list of likely customers for your self-employment enterprise. Whether your venture is to be a service or selling a product, identifying your intended customer is essential. Knowing who you will serve or sell to allows you to measure the size of your market and what you can reasonably expect as gross income. We call this the: **Marketing Plan.**

With your Marketing Plan established, the next thing to tackle is the financial aspects of your enterprise. Assuming your business will be a service, what kind of tools or office equipment will you be required to have that you don't already own? Purchasing a lot of equipment when you are low on cash and have been out of work should be reduced to an absolute minimum, or eliminated altogether. Should you be considering selling a product, then every effort should be made to negotiate terms on start-up inventory. We call this the: **Financial Plan.**

How are we going to do what we say we want to do? What will the day-to-day execution of our enterprise look like? Will we be on the phone for several hours cold-calling for prospects? Will we be going to local community meetings such as chambers of commerce? Will we be visiting various businesses and identifying our services or products? Laying out a routine daily schedule will help you utilize your time better, especially if you are planning on continuing to look for a job. We call this the: **Operating Plan.**

With all of this out of the way, our next part of the planning process is to prepare what we expect to achieve and how long we expect it to take to become self-sufficient as a self-employed entrepreneur.

Putting this into the plan allows us to measure the success of the venture. To do this, we must............

I WILL MAKE THIS WORK FOR ME BY:

Blank Space for your notes

AFFIRMATION: I am charged with enthusiasm as I work towards my new goals.

Set goals and thresholds

"The greater danger for most of us lies not in setting our aim too high and falling short; but in setting our aim too low, and achieving our mark." **Michelangelo**

Keeping the above quote in mind when you are making your plan, you should set a series of intermediate goals which we call thresholds, and at each level, you can give yourself a "pat on the back" for reaching that plateau before moving on to the next level--Some self-acknowledgement, like buying yourself a new pair of shoes or the jacket you have always wanted. Just something that says "atta-boy"/or "atta-girl".

Then you set your sights on the next threshold, doing this all along the way until you have reached your preliminary main goal of becoming self employed. From there, the ultimate goal becomes reaching the point where you have an income from your enterprise that is at least equal to, but most likely much higher than you were making when you were employed by someone else in a job you didn't like as much as what you will be doing.

I WILL MAKE THIS WORK FOR ME BY:

Blank Space for your notes

AFFIRMATION: I am committed to my goals and my success is assured.

You must be your best cheerleader and most severe critic

Waiting for someone else to cheer you on is fruitless. Chances are your wife or significant other is petrified that you will become a street beggar pushing a grocery cart if you pursue this crazy idea. Pay no attention. Believe in your dream and yourself with all of your inner strength. But don't be fool hardy.

Your idea must be doable and your goals reachable. I'm not talking here about convincing yourself that your idea is the best thing since sliced bread. Researching your idea or concept is very important to your success. Once you have decided where your talents and desires fit into your self-employment plan, the next step is checking out the market place. Will you have clients or customers for the service or product you plan to offer?

This subject was partially covered in the previous section, but now we must scrutinize everything you have put down in your plan and look for glitches in your thought processes. What will you charge for your product or service? Is your fee competitive with others in the field? When you have critiqued your plan thoroughly and are satisfied with the results, you're ready for the big test.

I WILL MAKE THIS WORK FOR ME BY:

Blank Space for your notes

AFFIRMATION: He can who thinks he can; He can't who thinks he can't.

One step at a time

Take it slowly and deliberately, moving through your plan thoughtfully, checking yourself all the way. You will make mistakes—we all do. The trick is a quick recovery and then another step forward. Read the reactions of your client/customer. Is he/she pleased? Dubious? Concerned?

There is no crime in asking for comments. As a matter of fact, most clients and customers will welcome your questions surrounding their satisfaction. When they know you are making sure they are pleased, you have assured them that you have their situation uppermost in your efforts to help resolve their issues. That's good customer service.

I WILL MAKE THIS WORK FOR ME BY:

Blank Space for your notes

AFFIRMATION: I will be persistent in all that I do.

Don't bank on your Banker

Maybe you are one of the few that have a personal relationship with your bank manager. Should you be one of those rare people, most likely he or she will try to talk you out of becoming self employed.

Bankers are not risk takers and they don't want their customers to risk their savings either. They think you might lose money, which reduces the money the bank has of yours that they can lend to others. That isn't good banking practice. And if you think you would like to borrow money…………

I WILL MAKE THIS WORK FOR ME BY:

Blank Space for your notes

AFFIRMATION: I focus on what is truly essential.

You will only get a loan when you don't need it.

Maybe you've had the experience already, or maybe you've heard someone say it that's had the experience, but contrary to what most banks are saying, they aren't loaning money to very small businesses in any large quantities and if or when they do, the borrower will be platinum plated in the credit department.

Remember most Bankers don't put their money at risk. You only need open the newspaper to see what has happened to those banks that have been risking their depositors money—they are either being shut down or rescued by the government. That's a whole other story.

However, should you decide you still want to talk to your banker, take your finished business plan to him or her, and sit down with the intent of at least getting advice (good or bad as it might be). Good advice is always welcome, and bad advice can always be ignored. Their egos will be pumped and you will have impressed them with your business plan even if they don't agree with it. And who knows? You could get lucky and a loan.

I WILL MAKE THIS WORK FOR ME BY:

Blank Space for your notes

AFFIRMATION: I have within me the power to do the most incredible things.

The power of networking

Networking is not new. Networking on the Internet is. But let's cover the art of networking before we talk about the Internet—and it is an art. In one form or another, you have been networking most of your life. Should you be a woman, you are a better net-worker than your male counter part. It's a gender thing, trust me.

The short version is: Networking is meeting with and communicating with a wide range of like-minded individuals who are, or may be involved with or interested in a similar business or community or social activities for the mutual benefit of all.

The long version is: **Business networking** is a socioeconomic activity by which groups of like-minded businesspeople recognize, create, or act upon business opportunities. A business network is a type of social network whose reason for existing is business activity.

There are several prominent business networking organizations that create models of networking activity that, when followed, allow the business person to build new business relationships and generate business opportunities at the same time. A professional network service is an implementation of information technology in support of business networking.

Many businesspeople contend business networking is a more cost-effective method of generating new business than advertising or public relations efforts. This is because business networking is a low-cost activity that involves more personal commitment than company money.

As an example, a business network may agree to meet weekly or monthly with the purpose of exchanging business leads and referrals with fellow members. To complement this activity, members often meet outside this circle, on their own time, and build their own one-to-one relationship with the fellow member.

Business networking can be conducted in a local business community, or on a larger scale via the Internet. Business networking websites have grown over recent years due to the Internet's ability to connect people from all over the world. Internet companies often set up business leads for sale to bigger corporations and companies looking for data sources.

Business networking can have a meaning also in the ICT domain, i.e. the provision of operating support to companies and organizations, and related value chains and value networks.

It [networking] refers to an activity coordination with a wider scope and a simpler implementation than pre-organized workflows or web-based impromptu searches for transaction counterparts (workflow is useful to coordinate activities, but it is complicated by the use of s.c. patterns to deviate the flow of work from a pure sequence, in order to compensate its intrinsic linearity; impromptu searches for transaction counterparts on the web are useful as well, but only for non-strategic supplies; both are complicated by a plethora of interfaces needed among different organizations and even between different IT applications within the same organization).

The above "long version" explanation was posted on Wikipedia. The short version is mine.

Whether using the long or short explanation, networking is the most essential, easiest and least expensive method of growing any business today.

With the added ability of using the Internet to reach out to a network of peers, potential client/customers and your ever-growing list of contacts, your exponential growth is almost assured. If you don't think this is true, just look at how fast Facebook and LinkedIn have grown since their start-up phase a few years ago.

I WILL MAKE THIS WORK FOR ME BY:

Blank Space for your notes

AFFIRMATION: My prosperity contributes to the prosperity of others.

Make a list of your friends & relatives

Start Here: (If you can't fit them all here, grab a blank page)

Blank Space for your notes

Make a list of former co-workers: (If you can't fit them all here, grab a blank page)

Blank Space for your notes

Make a list of stores & shops you & your family frequent: (If you can't fit them all here, grab a blank page)

Blank Space for your notes

Make a list of former school chums: (If you can't fit them all here, grab a blank page)

Blank Space for your notes

Now send all of the above the following letter:

(Snail-mail is preferred to e-mail and Priority Mail if you have the bucks—it won't get thrown in the trash without being read)

Dear_________

After searching for a job without success for the past____months, I have decided to create my own job.

I know this might sound risky, but I have to do something and I read a book titled "When You Can't find a JOB, Create One" and it's kind of a "How To" and Diary all in one. So I decided to follow what the book says. I have nothing to lose at this point.

As a result, I am creating my own JOB, by starting a business and I am looking for advice and assistance from anyone with similar experiences and the willingness to share.

Since this is a new business, I am not able to pay for your advice at this time, but I will tell all of my network friends that you have helped me.

The job I intend to create for myself is in the_______________ business.

As I build my business and marketing plan, I will be using the Internet to make contacts and build my network of potential clients and customers, so with this letter, I am asking you for names of people you think would be interested in sharing their name, address and e-mail address with me.

My promise to you and your friends is that I will not give their information to anyone, and will use their address only to communicate directly with them in the future.

Please call me at: xxx-xxx-xxxx or e-mail me at ____@________.___ for any additional information you may want. Thanks for your help.

I WILL MAKE THIS WORK FOR ME BY:

Blank Space for your notes

AFFIRMATION: I act with assurance, confidence and grace.

Using the Internet to help you grow

When properly used, the Internet is a powerful tool. Vast numbers of people; clients; customers; friends and relatives can be communicated with over a wide range of geographic locations in an instant. However, the medium can and is often abused. You do not want to be an abuser.

Businesses can circulate a newsletter as a way of keeping the company in front of current clients or customers and to generate potential business from their referrals. I have and currently use the newsletter as a business builder and to keep my current associates informed on a broad range of issues concerning them. That address is: http://archive.constantcontact.com/fs029/1101932703160/archive/1101955090741.html .

Articles can be easily uploaded from public domain sites and placed into a newsletter, by giving the source credit. A short tutorial on how this is done appears in this book on page 55 under the heading "Using Constant Contact to tell everyone what you are doing"

I WILL MAKE THIS WORK FOR ME BY:

Blank Space for your notes

AFFIRMATION: I am committed to results.

Establishing a Facebook© page (Cost: $0)

The phenomenal growth of Facebook© is clear evidence of the power of the Internet and its ability to reach around the world to what is currently 750 million people in seconds, with *any message you care to put out in public*. I emphasize the latter, because once you hit the send button on a public access site such as Facebook or LinkedIn, it will remain in cyber space for anyone in the world to view. So keep that in mind as you use this mode of communication in your business or personal life.

Step 1: Open up your Web browser

Step 2: Type in Facebook.com & follow the instructions

Step 3: Write the following message in your "Status" box:

I am creating my own JOB, by starting a __________ business and I am looking for advice and assistance from anyone with similar experiences and the willingness to share.

Since this is a new business, I am not able to pay for your advice at this time, but I will tell all of my network friends that you and your company have helped me. Thanks.

Establishing a LinkedIn© Page (Cost $0)

LinkedIn is a different type of networking, in that it focuses primarily on professionals in business and is a much more sophisticated structure. Also, LinkedIn is rapidly becoming a widely recognized site for job-seekers and companies looking for new employees. When filling out your Profile page, don't be bashful about blowing your own horn—remember, believing in yourself is essential. When you believe in yourself enough to tell the world how good you are, you aren't bragging, you are making a statement of fact.

Follow the process just as with Facebook©:

Step 1: Open up your Web browser

Step 2: Type in LinkedIn.com & follow the instructions.

Step 3: When the "Share" box appears repeat the Facebook© statement on page 60.

Once you have established Profile pages, start searching for "friends" on Facebook and "Contacts" on LinkedIn, working with both every day to expand your network. You will be surprised how quickly both resources will grow for you.

I WILL MAKE THIS WORK FOR ME BY:

Blank Space for your notes

AFFIRMATION: Every new decision I make becomes a new reality in my life.

Using Constant Contact© to tell everyone what you are doing **(Cost varies; starts at $15.00 Per/Month with a 60-day free trial)**

Constant Contact© is another indispensable tool that a business should not be without today. I have been using Constant Contact since it was first introduced, and would not want to be without it.

Beyond the program's primary function, which is to send all of your large "gang" e-mails without being kicked off by your Internet Service Provider (ISP), and maintaining your e-mail lists as they grow, there are easy to use, fully functional templates to design business letters, newsletters, flyers, bulletins and interactive messaging which appear professionally prepared, adding to your company's stature in the business community.

As soon as you begin building your network of e-mail addresses, putting Constant Contact to work for you is a must, in my view.

You can start by sending an e-mail with an explanation of what you have decided to do to create your job, what you are thinking of calling your new enterprise and asking for suggestions from people on your list.

Most everyone likes to be asked for their opinion. You will receive many good suggestions. Using them is your choice.

To get started, go to:

www.constantcontact.com on your web browser and when the page pops up, click on "sign-up". Once there you will see several options and pricing—the most important one, is "60-day Free Trial". That's what I did and have never been sorry.

During the free trial period, you can experiment with all of the various options and template choices for your best methods of communicating with your prospects and networking potentials.

You might also join one of the Constant Contact on-line user-seminars to help you get better acquainted. I have found the company's Customer Service responders to be exceptional at handling any of my problems.

Building a personal Web Page

Domain name registration about $10.00); Hosting varies and can be free with some companies; I use Go-Daddy for about $20 per month. www.godaddy.com

Web pages can be elaborate or simple, expansive or minimalist. They can be expensive to build or inexpensive, depending on how you go about it. For personal and new business start-ups, I highly recommend the do-it-yourself approach. That may startle you if you are not a "computer junkie" but it's not as difficult as you might think.

There are many programs you can buy to build a web page with that you can install on your computer, but I have found that by going on-line to Go-Daddy.com I can build and have a web site hosted extremely inexpensively with their "Web Site Tonight" template design process and be up and running in less than a day of effort.

Like Constant Contact, I have been using Go Daddy since its inception, and currently run five web sites with ease and few if any glitches. Any problems that do arise are quickly resolved with the company's exceptional customer service team.

Building your business web page (Cost: same as personal—see page 58)

While your personal web site should tell the world who you are, and how good you are at what you do, this is a more intimate view of you and your family, your hobbies and if possible a family tree going as far back as you can. Many times distant relatives or old school chums long forgotten will make contact with you when you least expect it.

Your business web page on the other hand is a different animal altogether. You want to look as professional as possible and have a site that is easy to navigate for the observer, and a web address that is easy to recognize and type.

As an example, my first website which I built in 1998 and still running is:

http://www.BillEffinger.com. That's simple.

I WILL MAKE THIS ALL WORK FOR ME BY:

Blank Space for your notes

AFFIRMATION: Every new decision I make becomes a new reality in my life.

Using the Internet to market your business

Having all of the tools is essential to ensure your success, but it's only part of the equation. Putting all of those tools to work for you is where the rubber meets the road.

So here's how we will begin your marketing campaign. And just so you know, you don't have to wait until you have hung out your shingle or opened your doors to your new enterprise. You will start marketing your business in the very beginning. As a matter of fact, if you notice, you have been doing preliminary marketing all along the way from the time you decided to use this book. That is of course if you have been using the book as it is intended to be used; A step-by-step "How to" and creative Diary along with a few coaching sessions. Assuming you have been doing so, you now should have:

1. A reasonable size e-mail list

2. A Facebook page

3. A LinkedIn page

4. An operating personal Web Page

5. An operating business Web Page

6. A Subscription to Constant Contact

I WILL MAKE THIS WORK FOR ME BY:

Blank Space for your notes

AFFIRMATION: I am inspired and have the power to accomplish everything I need to do.

Using Google Search© to research your Niche (Cost $0)

Researching your ideas before you start your business is essential to your success. But that's not where your research should end. I have found Google© to be one of the most important resources for gathering information on almost every subject you can think of. A click on the Google address bar after typing in a few words of the subject matter I am researching, inevitably results in a plethora of URL addresses with a wide range of pertinent information on the subject, company or person I am researching.

Google© is an unbelievable and indispensable tool for everyone in business today. However, a word of caution: just because it's on the internet and on the Google site, doesn't mean what you see is Gospel. Cross-checking two or three different URL addressed articles is always a good idea. Anyone can put anything out there, and once it's there, it's there forever right or wrong, true or false.

So Let's do it!

But first, some helpful websites for when you are creating your own job and launching your new Business:

http://www.sba.gov

http://www.startbreakingfree.com

http://www.sos.state.ia.us/business

http://www.legalzoom.com

http://www.nolo.com

http://jobsearch.monster.com

Please Note: *The Author neither endorses nor recommends the use of any information obtained on the above websites. This information is to be used for reference only at the sole discretion of the reader.*

I WILL MAKE THIS WORK FOR ME BY:

Blank Space for your notes

AFFIRMATION: I take full responsibility for everything I do and say.

There are also many franchise opportunities out there.

Franchising is a major industry in America but it isn't for everyone. However, unless you look into the possibilities you won't know if you are one of the potential franchisees or not. So I looked for and found some very good places to start looking on the web.

Here are some of the companies I found that you can peruse on your computer as you formulate your plans for becoming self-employed.

http://www.franchising.com
http://www.smallbusinessopportunity.com

http://www.franchisedirect.com
http://www.entrepreneur.com/business-opportunities/
http://www.smallbusinesssale.com

After putting this book to bed and printing several "Proof Copies" I was introduced to Roxanne Rapske, "The Franchise Genie" she calls herself.

Impressed with what she shared with me in a follow up meeting, I proposed that we delay the final publication until she could prepare some information for readers of the book. She agreed, and as a result, I am able to share with you The Franchise Genie's expertise on what she knows and how she works with her potential franchisees. What follows is an example of her approach she uses in helping people become successful business owners:

Interviewing a prospective Franchisee

When I'm speaking with someone for the first time, I spend about 15-30 minutes getting to know them and sharing my background.

I like to know what they've been doing, their interests, hobbies, what businesses they may have looked at or considered in the past.

Many times, if they have considered a business, it's in the food industry & it's something in the million+ dollar range without knowing it's that large of an investment.

If I happen to know the figures and share that with them, they are usually shocked. As part of this conversation, I like to find out if there is a spouse or partner and if so, "are they on board?"

This is huge. If they are NOT on board, it will be just about impossible for this candidate to move forward. They will get to the very end of the process and back out – and everyone's time will have been wasted. So, I feel it's a very important question.

Then I explain my 3–step process:

Step 1:

Complete my confidential Self-Assessment Profile. This is a 23 question worksheet that will cover in depth, your life circumstances, your career path, dreams and passions, management background, composition of net worth. This is your homework assignment to complete before we move to our next call. I'm going to ask you in your private quiet time to sit down and really think through the importance of each question.

For your reference, below are some questions to ask yourself that can help you assess your readiness to open a franchise as well as an overview of the franchise investigation process.

Questions to ask yourself

- What is your net worth?
- How much do you wish to invest?
- Do you require a specific level of annual income
- In what environment do you see yourself – retail, mobile or office?
- Are you interested in pursuing a particular field?
- Do you want a part-time or fulltime opportunity?
- How many hours are you willing to work?
- When do you want to work – hours, days of the week?
- Do you want to have employees?
- Do you want to have inventory?
- Do you prefer a cash business as opposed to one that must carry accounts receivable?
- Will franchise ownership be your primary source of income or will it supplement your current income?

Step 2:

In our second telephone appointment, I would like to go over your profile with you in real detail and have some dialog. This usually takes about an hour.

Step 3:

In our third phone call, I will select 3-5 concepts within my portfolio to present to you and explain to you the discovery process for each concept. I'd like to find something that really fits you like a glove. The Good News is there is "No Charge" to you for my Services! I am compensated directly by the franchise company. I work much like a corporate recruiter.

Within a week's time, I can get them in front of several franchise companies that make sense for them to review. I will stay with them through the entire process. If they have any questions along the way, I can help them.

Each franchise company has their own investigative processes, but most consist of the following key elements:

Step 1 - General Information
The franchisor will begin by providing you with overview information on the company (typically a brochure and video package).

Step 2 - The Franchise Disclosure Document
This document, commonly referred to as the FDD, is the F.T.C. mandated disclosure document that gives you a wealth of information about the franchisor.

Step 3 - Franchisee Calls and Visits
The most valuable source of information on any franchise system is the

existing franchisees. You need to plan on calling or visiting a number of the existing franchisees during your investigation

Though you want to find the overwhelming majority of franchisees to be happy and supportive of the franchisor, it is important to try to find an unhappy franchisee during your investigation.

The following list covers the principle areas you want to investigate during these calls:

- **Training Programs** - You need to determine how well the initial training programs and support prepared the franchisees for opening and running their business.
- **Opening Support** - How easy did the franchisor make the process of getting the first unit open and operating? Was there assistance in site selection, lease negotiation, construction and design assistance, financing assistance, permits or any other factors unique to getting this business up and operating?
- **Ongoing Support** - You want to know how effective the ongoing support services of the franchisor are in terms of helping franchisees deal with the problems that come up in the running of their business.
- **Marketing Programs** - Most franchisors collect marketing dollars from every franchisee into a pool that is spent to promote the brand. You need to know whether the franchisees are happy and supportive of the way this process is handled. Note: this is typically the area where you will find the most complaining in any franchise you examine.
- **Purchasing Power** - Does the franchisor use the collective buying power of the total system to get discounts on supplies and inventory beyond what an independent operator could achieve? This factor is one of the biggest advantages of joining a well-run franchise system and should offset much of the fee cost associated with being a franchisee.

- **Franchisor/Franchisee Relations** - Determine what the franchisees feel about the franchisor in general. Is the franchisor supportive, caring, focused on their success, responsive, effective, organized, and trustworthy? Make sure you have a good feeling about the values of the organization and that they are consistent with your values.
- **Investment** - The FDD will give you a wide dollar range for the investment required in the business. Use the franchisee discussions to narrow that down to a reasonable and conservative estimate of how much capital you will need to be successful in this franchise.
- **Earnings** - It is critical that you have a strong sense of just where the average unit is in terms of earnings. You should know the answers to the following questions: How much money does the typical unit make given a specified length of time in business? How soon does a typical unit start making money after opening? What is the range of answers for these questions? If you are simply not able to determine these answers to your satisfaction in your research, do not settle! Tell the franchisor of the problem and that you cannot proceed unless you have these answers.

It is always a good idea to bring up the subject of earnings as the last point in your franchisee visits. Most people are reluctant to discuss their income with strangers and you will find the franchisees are more willing to cover this subject after you have spent some time visiting with them.

Step 4 - Review the System Documentation

A strong franchise company will have documented their systems, operations and marketing programs in a concise and easy to use format for the reference of franchisees.

Step 5 - Meet the Franchisor

At some point in the process of investigation, you will want to have personal meetings with key personnel of the franchise company.

Step 6 - Make a Decision

If you have been diligent, the entire process outlined above will take about three to five weeks to complete. You now have all the information you need to determine if this franchise is right for you.

Roxanne Rapske

Franchisee & Distributor Recruitment

Office (760) 477-7075

Toll free (877) FRAN-4U-0 (372-6480)

www.thefranchisegenie.com

I WILL MAKE THIS WORK FOR ME BY:

Blank Space for your notes

AFFIRMATION: At every turn opportunity appears before me.

And what about your health care?

Assuming you are like most of us, health care is a major issue for yourself and your family. When you're out of a JOB it usually means you don't have health care, or if you do, it's a major expense and doesn't take care of everything that can go wrong.

The following website is a complete "everything you ever wanted to know and how to get good Health Care coverage" bundled into one single place, which has been provided by the **Henry J. Kaiser Family Foundation** as a community service.

I suggest you punch these addresses into your browser address bar and study them carefully. I believe you will find it to be extremely beneficial and worth more than what you paid for this book: http://healthreform.kff.org/the-basics. Below is a copy of a chart from the Kaiser Foundation home page

How People Get Coverage Under the Affordable Care Act

The Affordable Care Act will reduce the number of people without health insurance by expanding eligibility for Medicaid and providing tax credits that make insurance more affordable for people buying coverage on their own through new health insurance Exchanges. The Congressional Budget Office projects that 32 million more people will have insurance by 2019. Find out who gets covered and how with this simple flowchart.

View full-sized version (.pdf)

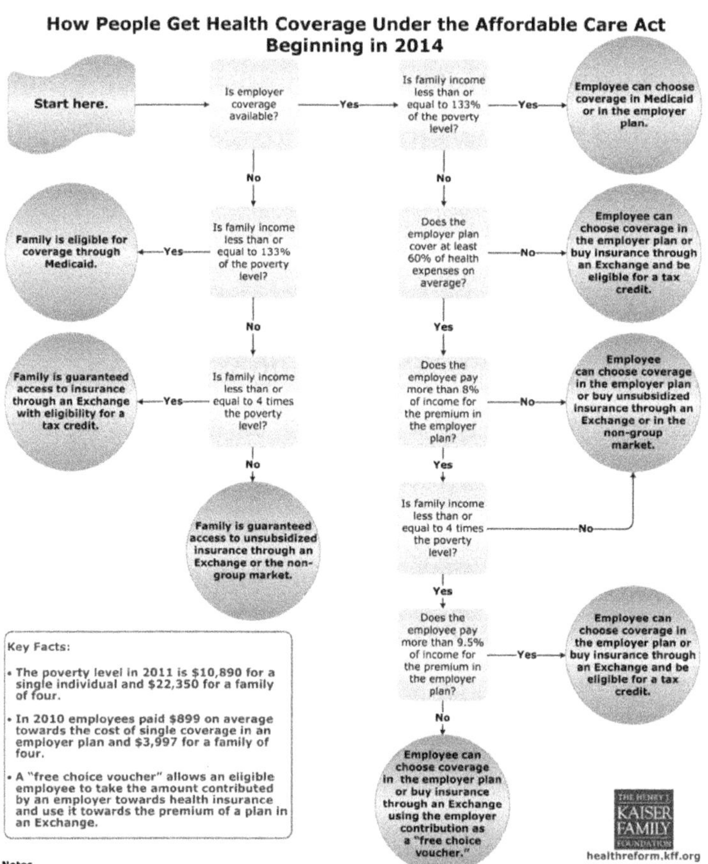

Also check this one out: http://www.healthcare.gov

Here is an article from their Home Page:

Important Information for Small Businesses Owners

Posted September 07, 2011

By Richard Sorian, Assistant Secretary for Public Affairs

If you're a small business owner, there are a few deadlines approaching that you won't want to miss in order to help provide health coverage for your employees.

As you might know, if you have up to 25 employees, pay average annual wages below $50,000, and provide health insurance, you may qualify for a small business tax credit of up to 35% (up to 25% for non-profits) to offset the cost of your insurance. This will bring down the cost of providing insurance.

In order to take advantage of these tax credits, you must file by a certain date. Here are two important tax filing deadlines in coming weeks that you should be aware of:

- **September 15.** Corporations that file on a calendar year basis and requested an extension to file to September 15 can calculate the small employer health care credit on Form 8941 and claim it as part of the general business credit on Form 3800, which they would include with their corporate income tax return.
- **October 17.** Sole proprietors who file Form 1040 and partners and S-corporation shareholders who report their income on Form 1040 have until October 17 to complete their returns. They would also use Form 8941 to calculate the small employer health care credit and claim it as a general business credit on Form 3800, reflected on line 53 of Form 1040.

The Department of Health and Human Services (HHS), along with the IRS, wants to make sure that businesses who qualify take advantage of the credit. In order to get the word out, there is a big outreach effort that will include IRS YouTube videos in English, Spanish and American Sign Language. Targeted e-mails and tweets will be sent to the small business community and tax preparers. The goal is to remind employers about the upcoming extension deadlines and also provide details on other important information about the credit, including:

- **Businesses who have already filed can still claim the credit:** For small businesses that have already filed and later determine they are eligible for the credit, they can always file an amended 2010 tax return. Corporations use Form 1120X and individual sole proprietors use Form 1040X
- **Businesses without tax liability this year can still benefit:** The Small Business Jobs Act of 2010 provided that for Tax Year 2010, eligible small businesses may carry back unused general business credits (including the small employer health care tax credit) five years. Previously these credits could only be carried back one year. Small businesses that did not have tax liability to offset in 2010 should still evaluate eligibility for the small business health care tax credit in light of this expanded carry back opportunity.
- **Business that couldn't use the credit in 2010 can claim it in future years:** Some businesses that already locked into health insurance plan structures and contributions for 2010 may not have had the opportunity to make any needed adjustments to qualify for the credit for 2010. So these businesses may be eligible to claim the credit on 2011 returns or in years beyond. Small employers can claim the credit for 2010 through 2013 and for two additional years beginning in 2014.

The Administration will also continue to work with and encourage private-sector outreach. For example, a number of Blue Cross Blue Shield plans implemented a wide variety of innovative outreach initiatives to promote the program and encourage small employers to offer insurance coverage to their workers. Blue Cross Blue Shield of Kansas City is a leading innovator with a promotion campaign built around the H&R Block tax calculator and the small business tax credit on its site www.BlueKCTaxcredit.com. Since April 2010, they have enrolled over 9,000 new members covered in over 400 new employers. Thirty-eight percent of these employers previously did not offer insurance.

Additional information about eligibility requirements and calculating the credit can be found on the Small Business Health Care Tax Credit for Small Employers page of IRS.gov.

I WILL MAKE THIS WORK FOR ME BY:

Blank Space for your notes

AFFIRMATION: I am changing my old and limiting beliefs.

For Our Veterans

The government has provided financial assistance to our Veterans for new business start ups. Listed below are some of the links and explanations of the available programs.

Using this book as a guide along with one or more of the government programs to assist, you will be well on your way to successful self-employment.

1. http://www.vetbiz.gov/

Vetbiz.gov is the Department's internet site developed to support Veterans interested in participating in VA's Veteran-owned small business (VOSB) Verification Program.

The principal purposes of this site are to communicate information about the verification process; to assist Veteran business owners in registering their business in the Secretary's Database of Veteran-owned small businesses and to provide a vehicle for VA contracting officers to easily identify service-disabled Veteran-owned small businesses and VOSBs for procurement opportunities.

This site is managed and maintained by the Center for Veterans Enterprise (CVE), a program office within the Department's Office of Small and Disadvantaged Utilization (OSDBU). The CVE is specifically responsible for: managing the Vendor Information Pages (VIP) database and managing the VOSB Verification Program.

2. http://www.sba.gov/about-offices-content/1/2985

SBA's Office of Veterans Business Development is responsible for liaison with the Veterans business community; for policy analysis and reporting; for acting as an Ombudsman for Veterans in Small Business Administration programs, for providing business training, counseling and assistance, and for overseeing the Federal procurement programs for Veteran and Service-Disabled Veteran-Owned small businesses.

http://www.navoba.com/aboutus.aspx

http://www.ehow.com/list_6746951_veteran_owned-business-grants.html

Veteran Entrepreneurship Support Grant

- The Veteran Entrepreneurship Support Grant is sponsored by the Veterans Corporation and offers funding to help veterans who are starting a business, or who already own a business and need extra financial assistance. Grant amounts vary depending upon financial need and availability.

  National Veterans Business Development Corporation

  P.O. Box 220

  Oxford, Maryland 21654

  info@veteranscorp.org

  202-349-0860

  veteranscorp.org

The McCormick Foundation

- The McCormick Foundation has grant opportunities for veterans who are trying to re-enter civilian life and experiencing various financial difficulties associated with re-assimilation into civilian society. The grant offers funds to veteran entrepreneurs who need startup funds, or those who are experiencing hardship within already established business endeavors.

  McCormick Foundation

  205 North Michigan Avenue

Suite 4300

Chicago, IL 60601

312-445-5000

Info@MccormickFoundation.org

mccormickfoundation.org

VetFran

- VetFran supports veterans who wish to buy franchising businesses around the United States. Aside from helping with initial franchising costs, VetFran offers support to existing franchise owners through grants, loans and other scholarship programs in the hopes of increasing veteran owned franchises throughout the United States. The grant is sponsored by the International Franchise Association and is available to honorably discharged or retired U.S. veterans.

International Franchise Association

1501 K Street, N.W., Suite 350

Washington, D.C. 20005

202-628-8000

franchise.org

Center for Veteran Enterprise

- The Center for Veteran Enterprise was created by the U.S. Department of Veteran Affairs to help veterans entering the business world and to provide informational and fiscal support to veteran-owned businesses throughout the United States. In addition to low-interest loan programs for business owners, like the Patriot Express loan, the center also provides grant funding.

U.S. Department of Veterans Affairs

The Center for Veterans Enterprise (CVE)

810 Vermont Avenue, N. W.

Washington, D.C. 20420

vip@mail.va.gov

www.vetbiz.gov

Read more: Veteran-Owned Business Grants | eHow.com http://www.ehow.com/list_6746951_veteran_owned-business-grants.html#ixzz1XWPS6j84

I WILL MAKE THIS WORK FOR ME BY:

Blank Space for your notes

AFFIRMATION: I deserve to be prosperous and successful.

I have practiced what I preach

Since my Honorable Discharge from the United States Navy in December of 1950 and continuing for 61 years, I have never been out of a job, whether employed by a company or being self-employed, and I have never drawn one day of Unemployment Insurance.

Jobs I have created for myself have varied widely, some requiring physical labor and others mostly sales based or consultative in nature, but there has always been personal income for me and my family. Neither I nor my family have ever missed a meal or been without a roof over our heads.

A few of my self-employment stints have not been the raging successes that I would have liked, and there were a couple that were downright failures. But I never gave up, I just moved on.

My personal income over the past 61-years has ranged from low, blue collar hourly wages, to medium-high executive level salaries. For most of my working life I have managed to do what I like to do, sometimes doing what I had to do. Some people might call this "luck"—I call it perseverance and creativity.

I have also managed to intersperse community service (which I highly recommend) and political involvement with my employment along with being able to pursue my hobbies of: Water Sports; Skiing; Golf; Painting; Writing and Speaking.

Listed on the following page are some jobs I have had either as an employee or being self-employed, during my adult years, sometimes overlapping when I was both self-employed and working for someone at the same time.

My Employment History

- A Good Humor Man **1950- (one month)**
- Apprentice Carpenter 19**50-1953**
- Journeyman Carpenter 19**53-1955**
- Northrop Aircraft **1953-1957**
- S&S Construction Company **1957-1960**
- Shapell Industries **1972-1980**

Businesses I have started, operated and sold:

- Speedy-Quick Delivery Service 19**51-1952**
- Boulevard Saw Shop **1953-1955**
- Framing Contractor **1954-1956**
- Alamitos Belmont Corporation (Builder) **1956-1970**
- Valencia Liquors **1966 to 1972**
- Huntington Harbor Liquors **1968 to 1972**

- Valley View Appaloosa Ranch, (A horse breeding and training ranch) **1972 to 1981***
- New Dimensions for Living (Builder/Developer) **1980 to 1985**
- Techno-Data Construction Software **1985 to 1987**
- Bird Construction Software **1987 to 1991**
- Marketing & Management Consultant **1992 to Present**

***Note:** I was also President of Shapell Industries of San Diego, a subsidiary of a NYSE company during this same time period.

Community Service Activities:

- Member, Buena Park, CA Jaycees: 19**56 to 1959**
- Member, Buena Park, CA City Council: **1957 to 1959**
- Mayor, City of Buena Park, CA: **1957 to 1959**
- Member, City of Escondido, CA Housing Advisory Commission: **1997**
- Chairman, Community Oversight Commission, San Marcos, CA: **May 2011 to Present**

Now it's time to create *your* Plan

The following pages are meant to get you started on creating your plan for self-employment. Whether you intend to be a one-person operation or start a small business, as you have observed while reading this book, to be effective your plan must be in writing.

You can make your plan as detailed or as brief as you wish, but put it down on paper and commit to it. And remember, just because you commit to your plan, it is not a static, "cast in concrete" never to be changed instrument. It is a living; growing dynamic thing that can and should be adjusted with the fickle moves of the market place.

My Self Employment Plan

My Executive Summary:

Blank Space for your notes

AFIRMATIONS: I demonstrate excellence within me

My Marketing Plan:

Blank Space for your notes

AFFIRMATION: I move forward eagerly while embracing the now.

My Operating Plan:

Blank Space for your notes

AFFIRMATION: I am determined to follow through until finished.

My Financial Plan:

Blank Space for your notes

AFFIRMATION: I recommit to my highest goals.

In Summary

A few things to remember: First, a Plan is just that—a Plan. It is not meant to be cast in concrete. We live in a dynamic world that is ever changing. Your plan is a flexible, living document that can and should be adjusted as circumstances change in the market place as they inevitably will.

Next, there are currently 14-million people in the same situation as you are right now—out of a JOB and no prospects of getting one soon. You happen to be one of them that by acquiring this book, have decided to do something about it. By so doing, you have already increased your chances of rising above the tide of desolation. You have decided to become the master of your fate.

Now listen to others whom have gone before you and taken the leap into self employment successfully.

As I mentioned earlier, the following words of wisdom and encouragement are offered in the spirit they are given by some very successful people who have each started their own businesses at least once, many of whom I have had the good fortune of having been associated with for the past forty-odd years, and some, a few years less, both as colleagues and friends of a lasting duration.

I asked each of these individuals to share a few words on the trepidations they may have had before jumping into the self-employment world and the exultation of their successes:

Some words from a few who took the plunge

John Robbins:

I started my first real business at age 39 and I still remember both the fear and elation surrounding my decision. My reasoning was based upon the simple fact that we only get one chance at this life and I could spend it all working for someone else, watching them reap the rewards, or step up and take my shot.

I also knew the longer I procrastinated the more difficult the decision would become and as each day passed my courage would diminish like a losing football team in the fourth quarter!

Mortgage Banking is an interest rate cyclical business and I also knew there was a real chance I would not succeed if the economy were to slide into a recessionary cycle before I built the capital necessary to build a real cushion. Since that day in 1986 I have built and sold three companies and never looked back other than to learn from the many mistakes I made along the way. The American Dream is alive and well, ready to reward those who embrace the opportunity.

Every day we read about success stories created by average people whose only assets were a dream and a little courage. For the entrepreneur no country provides more opportunity for success!

Think about this, what do you really have to lose, a little time and some invested capital but the reality is that you can always go back and work for wages to rebuild your nest egg for a second shot! Most millionaires made their fortune after failing at least once! Your time is now and the only way you lose is to never take the chance!

John Robbins

American Residential Mortgage Corporation

American Residential Investment Trust

American Mortgage Network

Current President-CEO Bexil American Mortgage Corp.

****

Tom Dobron

I started my first homebuilding company in 1983 after being laid off by a large California building company in 1983. The USA was in a major recession with interest rates above 15%. I had 2 small children with a third on the way. I was 32 years old.

I basically put our family at financial risk however I knew that I had learned valuable lessons from my past employers both good and bad. That gave me the confidence that I could make a reasonable living working for myself and not rely on others to impact my financial future and it worked.

It took a lot of hard work every day and surrounding myself with intelligent self starters when I could hire them to further the success of the company.

So do not be afraid to hire someone smarter than you and make sure to pay them for a job well done. Remember there is a big difference between a risk taker and a great employee who helps grow your company.

I am proud to be a contributor to Bill's book. He mentored me when he was the president of the company that eventually laid me off. Thanks Bill.

Tom Dobron

****

Sharon Jenkins

As my older daughter was approaching high school graduation I realized I had to figure out what I would do "when I grew up". I was 47 and hadn't worked a full-time job for close to 20 years. I had volunteered in the schools and worked as a part-time Accountant, but thinking about what I might do after both my daughters graduated seemed overwhelming.

I decided to go into business for myself because I would have control over how I ran my business. It was 2005 and the real estate industry was booming. I decided to obtain my Realtor's license. I had worked as an Accountant for a mortgage company and felt comfortable in real estate.

Within a couple years of figuring out what I would do "when I grew up" I thought I might have made the wrong choice. I jumped into real estate and then the bubble burst. It was poor timing, but I was determined to be one of the lucky ones who would make it through.

Fast forward several years later.....while it hasn't been easy I persevered through the tough times by staying in touch with my clients/sphere of influence and working hard to exceed their expectations.

As you decide what you want to do "when you grow up" or what to do to survive during difficult times try to find something that you truly love, create a consistent marketing plan and don't give up when the going gets tough. Easier said than done, but doable!

Sharon Jenkins

Realtor©, North County Associated Brokers

****

Amir Iravani

I started my first business back in 1978. I was 12 years old at the time.

My incredible business idea was hatching chicken eggs and selling the chicks.

I was at my friend's house when I overheard their family talking about getting rid of an egg incubator. I immediately saw a potential opportunity to incubate eggs, sell the chicks and make a lot of money. I purchased the incubator and took it home, where my father immediately told me I better not bring that thing into the house.

Of course I had to continue with my business plan even if it meant getting in trouble. I took some of our eggs and some eggs that I bought and set up my new incubating business in the basement of our house. It wasn't long before my father found out, but luckily my mother intervened and bought me enough time to hatch three chicks before having to shut the business down.

I have had at least a dozen different start-up businesses between now and then.

My current business is NK Towing & Roadside Service, Which began in 2004 when I was working for one of my ex-wife's nephews at his new junkyard. I had several successful businesses and he wanted me to evaluate his business and find where he could improve to be more efficient. I found he had many customers wanting to sell their junk cars that he needed to pick up. He also needed to move the old vehicle chassis's out, to make room for the new vehicles coming in. He was having to pay tow companies to provide this service. I proposed if he purchased his own tow truck, he could easily pay the payment and immediately see a cost savings.

The nephew stated that his parents owned a tow company in another city and he didn't want to be in the tow business and suggested that I do it. I asked him and his parents a lot of questions about towing, went out and purchased a used truck and stated my own business. I never looked back and have been adding equipment and clients ever since.

If you are waiting for the perfect time to start your own business, you will be waiting a very long time. You need to evaluate what you have to work with, find your own opportunity. Be creative, don't be afraid of hard work and then slowly keep adding to your business one step at a time, solving one problem at a time. Persistence will eventually pay off.

A. Iravani

President, NK Towing, Inc.

****

MIKE ROSTON

I started my first business in 1971 at age 21 immediately after obtaining my California Real Estate Broker's License. I set up a small residential brokerage business and had some quick short term success but got humbled by a recession.

After an intense three year position under the guidance of Bill Effinger, I was anxious to prove to myself that I could create, lead and succeed. I chose to leave the security of a regular paycheck and joined two other colleagues and started a homebuilding company. Since then I have formed numerous other homebuilding and land development companies and have always enjoyed the ever changing challenges of being in control of my own destiny. I enjoy knowing that every day can bring solutions to yesterday's problems.

These certainly are the most challenging times my generation has experienced and the world has changed dramatically since I first went into business, but the formula for personal growth and development has NOT.

New businesses are still being created every day. Ask yourself what you can do and what you want to do. Wake up everyday with a plan and the energy to make it happen and it will.

Mike Roston

President, The Roston Southwest Companies

****

Jim Silverwood

I was intrigued by the allure of being my own boss.

In my early years I grew up in the construction trades, first as a laborer carrying lumber, then with bags as a an apprentice carpenter, shortly afterward a carpenter, then on to being a foreman (at only 22 years old) finally a superintendent.

Interacting with senior management and owners of development companies taught me many lessons, and frankly I looked at them and thought I could also be an owner or boss of a company.

Of course I was young and naive but it turned out I was correct. My jumping off point was taking a leap of faith and beginning my first development of four townhomes in Southern California.

In the development business timing is especially important. Seeking my first construction loan and being laughed out of major bank offices and later locating a small Thrift and Loan that charged an arm and a leg, but who nonetheless committed to my financing. Certainly there were many, many long hours in the early days.

I can remember working on those townhomes from just after dawn to dusk, then the paperwork each night to make sure the sub contractors were paid, then up the next day and the same thing over again. Now only in my mid twenties it turned out to be a success and I never looked back.

You will rise and succeed or fail through your own business decisions, and although it may at times be nerve-wracking it is also very, very satisfying.

Jim Silverwood

President, Affirmed Housing Group

****

Ruth Ko Roston

In 1957 at the age of 9 I got a job in a local Beauty shop sweeping up hair and cleaning the shampoo bowls, I worked for tips. Then at the age of 11, I started the first weed pulling business in our neighborhood. I charged 75 cents an hour or whatever I could get (I was very grateful for tips) I tried to get a paper route but they only hired boys, so I applied as a boy ... But was soon found out and fired.

At 15 I quit school and ran away from home with a Hawaiian show, and was able to travel and see the world. In 1965 At 17 I started a small Christmas tree lot with a borrowed $1,000 investment (from my step-dad Sollie) I made $10,000.

Because Of my ethnic look and Dancing capabilities I landed some TV Commercials and returning roles on the Beverly Hillbillies and Charlie's Angels.. To this day I still get residuals from both (97 cents per episode).

For the next 4 years I danced at the Tahitian Terrace at Disneyland , continued to do commercials (Kellogg's corn flakes, Continental airlines, Pan Am airlines) to name a few. My former husband and I in 1972 opened a shoe store in Lake Forest (Ko's Footwear) we had two locations

San Juan Capistrano and Lake Forest... We remained in business for 4 years.

In 1976 I started at Orange Coast magazine as an account executive ......worked my way through every department, at times there was no money for payroll so I received stock to stay.... The owner at the time went into personal bankruptcy.

In the early 90's I mortgaged my house , used all my savings, went to the bank with the magazines receivables and borrowed the money to buy his shares out of bankruptcy (very gutsy) the last $50,000 needed I borrowed on my credit cards... Fast forward to 2007; I sold Orange Coast Magazine. Reinventing myself in 2008, I have become an artist.

So, if there is a nugget of inspiration to be had. It does not matter what your education is, or whatever your humble beginnings are, stop blaming your others for what they did, or did not do. Make a plan, stay flexible and move forward.....

Ruth Ko Roston

****

I am very proud and honored to have been able to share some experiences with the people on the preceding pages and then watching them successfully grow their businesses.

I look forward to the opportunity of coaching and mentoring readers of this book as you take your first steps into becoming self employed.

Jump in—The Water's fine!

Suggested Reading

The following books have great insights for the reader when starting and building a new business. I highly recommend obtaining them and putting them in your reference library as you begin your new life as a self employed Entrepreneur.

- **The Seven Habits of Highly Effective People by Stephen Covey**

- **The E-Myth by Michel E. Gerber**

- **The One Minute Manager by Kenneth Blanchard**

Note:

Affirmations were accessed on the Google Page of "I'm In" and attributed to Ken Leonard. Some were modified by this author.

Author's Page

Author Bill Effinger

From the author: "My son-in-law Glenn Karrmann, made the observation that my writing this book and building its companion website is actually a metaphor for the book itself, as I am basically starting a coaching business with the book and the website. My son Brian insisted that I put Glenn's astute observation in the book, so here it is with my thanks to both of them.

Bill Effinger

Reviews

Bill Effinger in this book provides an excellent outline for structuring your thinking about starting a business. Employment today is very uncertain, and as Bill points out in the book, impossible for many individuals, given the nature of business today. Rather than accepting being unemployed or underemployed, this book provides guidance on how you can take control of your life by utilizing your life skills and knowledge to start a business. We all have something of value to give to the marketplace and this book provides a process for capitalizing upon that Value.

Dr. Dennis Guseman

Former Dean of the College of Business Administration, California State University San Marcos

****

In the nearly four decades I've known Bill Effinger, I've watched him move from the very top level of corporate management to a highly successful and well-respected entrepreneur and consultant. So, I'd be hard-pressed to identify a better person to give disciplined counsel to those in career transition on how to succeed and prosper.

Bill has done exactly that in "When You Can't Find a JOB, Create One!" This is far more than a written pep talk; it is a *"work* book" in every sense of the term. It starts by helping the reader conduct a personal inventory in writing of his or her own characteristics – likes and dislikes, experiences, values, etc. – all important self observations to take into account before launching out into the deep of today's marketplace.

Being accountable to one's self is key to success in any major endeavor, including creating a new business. Readers won't get very far in Bill's workbook – or in any venture of self employment – if they're not willing to take what they learn from Bill and apply it to a listing of their personal assets and a written plan.

"When You Can't Find a JOB, Create One!" is a must for anyone who's serious about bettering themselves in today and tomorrow's economy.

Dick Daniels

Former Vice Mayor, City of Escondido, CA

Newspaper Columnist & Public Relations Consultant

Remember my pledge to you: Just open your browser on your computer to **<u>www.jobcreator.biz</u>** and click on the "Hey Coach" tab with your quick questions and you will receive a response within 48 hours. Extended Coaching sessions are available on a quoted fee basis.

Bill Effinger

Principal,

New Century Consulting

New Century Publishing

100 E. San Marcos Blvd. Suite 400

San Marcos, California 92078

www.ingramcontent.com/pod-product-compliance
Lightning Source LLC
Chambersburg PA
CBHW032010190326
41520CB00007B/417

* 9 7 8 0 6 1 5 5 3 7 9 6 2 *